SUBMISSION IS NOT THE ENEMY: A

KEY FACTOR TO A HEALTHY

RELATIONSHIP

COVER DESIGNED BY: MARIAH

EVANS

PRIOR WRITTEN PERMISSION OF

THE PUBLISHER.

ALLMIGHTY PUBLISHING

ISBN 978-0-9982701-0-4

WOMEN'S ISSUES REGARDING
SUBMISSION

If you are a woman reading this
book, you more than likely view
submission as this outdated, degrading,
unnecessary, belittling term and practice
that needs to be done away with
forever. You most likely feel as though
any woman that is in alliance with being
submissive to her man/husband is either
insecure, desperate for love, or
completely unaware of her value. In
your mind, only a woman that does not
respect herself and notice her power as
a woman, would ever submit to her man

in any capacity. You view submissive women as weak & inferior that need to get a grip on reality, because after all, *NO* man is worth submitting to. Not even your husband.

Well, I'm here to tell you women that possess that mentality that you are absolutely wrong, and that's probably the reason why your relationships up to this point are either failing or have failed miserably. You don't realize that submissive women are not only the women that are being sought after by "high-caliber" men, but that submissive women understand the power in being submissive. Submission is a powerful,

key component to a healthy relationship.

It gives structure and balance to our

unions by stripping away the power

struggle and giving each other the

opportunity to take direction and give

direction respectfully and effectively.

The problem is that many of us have the

wrong idea of what submission is

supposed to be in regards to a

relationship, or we practice submission

entirely wrong.

Submission is not intended to be this

competitive, dictator type of dynamic,

but rather a beautiful and harmonic

dance between a couple in a strong, loving, healthy, beautiful union. A woman being submissive to her man shows that she understands his needs, loves him, and most importantly trusts him to lead, teach, and guide her in the right direction. The issue comes into place when this dance that's supposed to be harmonic and beautiful, turns into a battle of the sexes, where one wants to be the controller and rule over the other party. When this becomes the objective, the relationship is not healthy and is not displaying what submission is supposed to embody. Submission should not feel nor be forceful and degrading. It should feel and be

effortless, harmonic, and

complimentary.

Now I know you are probably

sitting there with your face frowned up

thinking to yourself, *" does this chick

even know the definition of submission;

because what she is describing is not

that."* In fact, you probably went to

google to back up your claim and saw

the definition of submission as *"1.the

action or fact of accepting or yielding to*

a superior force or to the will or authority

of another person."

The word that probably stuck out

immediately to you was *"superior"*,

which left a bad taste in your mouth

further stating your claim of how I'm a

looney-tune that does not know that

submission is a degrading thing in and

of itself. But what if I told you that, that's

essentially what we have to do in our

relationships in order to bring balance,

structure, and order?

Now, I'm not saying that a man is

more valuable, important, and has

complete control over his woman, or

vice versa. But I do feel as though we should be regarding each other in certain ways when it comes to our relationships; giving each other permission to take the lead when it better suits them, without resistance.

Submission in regards to a relationship should reflect a man and a woman being able to take the lead and follow when need be, while respecting each other's roles and positions in their relationship.

Any couple in a loving, healthy, strong, lasting relationship or marriage, knows and understands that submission is not to be taken as a man being toxic and degrading to his woman, and making her feel as if she is not valuable and beneath him. *(Nor should a woman be doing this to her man.)* Instead, it is to be seen as a woman being able to cater to, follow the lead of, and go with the flow of a man of true value and substance that truly embodies what it is to be a Leader, Teacher, Nurturer, Provider, and Protector.

Now I know you have a problem with the definition of submission listed previously, but lets go back and see how it can be applied to our relationships. Being able to be *accepting and yielding* to the suggestions or requests from your significant other, is a great quality that one can possess. How toxic and dysfunctional would our relationships and marriages be if we met every request and every suggestion from our partner with resistance and force, and never was accepting or yielding to what they had to say? It would lead to constant clashing and arguments and nothing would ever get accomplished. Thus, there is no need for us to feel that just because we are being receptive, understanding, doing what our partner would like from us, or what they may deem to be something of great value or benefit for us to do,

somehow makes us weak and inferior.

In fact, it not only makes our relationship

stronger, but it also makes our partner

even more loving and appreciative of us,

and in turn makes them want to

reciprocate and pour back into us. This

is where that beautiful and harmonic

dance that I keep referring to manifests

itself into our relationship.

When a man feels as though his

woman respects, honors, and obliges to

him, this creates a deeper and more

loving connection that he has for his

woman. This plays into his masculinity

and gives him more sense of responsibility, because he knows that he has a woman that trusts him, and that is relying on him to make the right judgment calls. The only issue with submission is when a woman is trusting, yielding to, accepting, loving, and catering to the *wrong* man.

WHAT TYPE OF MAN SHOULD BE SUBMITTED TO

Ladies, I'm here to let you all know that submission is *not* the enemy in your relationship. The enemy of your relationship is the *quality* of the man *you are choosing* to be submissive towards. You cannot be submissive towards toxic, dead-beat men, then get upset when things start to crumble due to you feeling weak, used, and taken for granted. Before we give submissive qualities to a man, he must first show and prove to us his value. We cannot just be submissive to a man simply because he is a male that we just so happen to be with. In fact, if he is a man that is not worthy of submission, we shouldn't be with him, entertain him, or give him our time, energy, and attention, in the first place.

The qualities a man must possess

in order to deem him worthy enough of a

relationship, let alone submission,

consist of leadership, trustworthiness,

knowledge, wisdom, understanding,

strength, power, nurturing, providing,

protecting, teaching, self-discipline,

good work-ethic, organization,

faithfulness, love, compassion,

dominance, authority, intelligence, etc.

If a man does not have these qualities,

he should not even be entertained. Too

often, us women jump into relationships

with men based upon his *potential* to

embody certain characteristics, versus

what he is actively showing and proving

to us. This is a set up for failure and

disappointment because, that man very

well may never become the man that

you need for him to be, or embody the

characteristics that a true leader,

provider, and protector are supposed to

have.

As women, we must be wise

enough to know and understand that all

men are not the same, and to stop

boxing them all in due to the poor

treatment of the men that we were once

involved with. If you were previously in a

relationship with a man that treated you badly that you just so happened to be submissive to, the problem was not the act of being submissive. The problem was that poor quality man that you made the poor decision to be involved with in that way, and you must understand that poor quality man *(or men)* do not represent the whole. Thus, it is foolish and unwise to say that no man should be submitted to based upon the immature and hurtful actions of a handful from your past.

I've heard the many arguments of women that feel that submission is a dangerous and foolish game to play. Many of them have valid points, but completely negate the fact that those men that it may be dangerous and foolish to submit to, were low vibrational men that did not have the above mentioned qualities in the first place. If a man is being overly possessive, toxic, demeaning, controlling, or abusive in any way, shape, or form; he does not deserve the luxury of having a woman that is nurturing, loving, catering, or submissive to him, because he will do nothing but abuse it and use it against her. This is why it is very important for women to know who is worthy enough to be submissive to.

WHY WE HAVE PROBLEMS WITH SUBMISSION

Growing up, many of us women, especially Black women, have never been exposed to a healthy relationship between men and women. In most instances, the male figure is completely absent, or is present, but does not showcase the leadership, provider, and protector role. This hinders women from being able to truly understand what position a man must play in their lives as women, and what traits a man must possess in order to be in their lives in the first place. Thus, we grow up thinking that the low-quality men are the ones that we are supposed to be involved with romantically and raise our families with, because those are the types of men that we were exposed to.

This leads women into an even bigger issue of feeling the need to be the leaders, providers, and protectors of their households and families, because the men they were exposed to were not handling their duties and obligations as men. This may force a lot of women into a more dominating role that they do not want to get out of, because deep down inside they do not trust their men to handle their responsibilities, make the right decisions, and lead them in the right direction. Due to this, many women may start to treat men like children, or warp our minds into being submissive to weak-minded men that cannot lead us.

That brings me to the men. Men suffer from the same type of dilemma; only they are trying to emulate what they see and don't see from the men around them. Growing up, many men, especially Black Men, are constantly seeing men that are absent from the household, or they see men treating and/or talking to women in disrespectful and degrading manners. They then internalize that and believe this to be okay. This introduces into the young males mind, that it is fine for men to be absent and uninvolved with their families, and to be weak or disrespectful towards women. Young men are not being shown or taught how to have leadership, provider, and protector type qualities from their poor upbringings, and are also being exposed to mothers and other female family members, playing a more powerful role, which can

also add more confusion to the males as

far as their position in a male and

female relationship.

Men and women are not on the

same accord when it comes to the roles

of what a man and a woman are

supposed to demonstrate. This puts us

at odds and makes us feel that we are in

constant competition with one another &

not compatible with one another. Men

and women feeling the need to

constantly compete and defeat each

other makes it extremely difficult for us

to understand one another and build

upon solid, loving foundations. We need

to go back to the drawing board and

figure out what the rules and standards

need to consist of for both men and

women to collaborate effectively in a

healthy relationship. We can no longer

continue on with the destructive and

divisive ways and actions of men

against women and vice versa.

MEN WITH THE WRONG IDEA

ABOUT SUBMISSION

So often I hear toxic men talk about how women are beneath men, and how women are supposed to obey and bow down to men, no matter what that man does or doesn't do for that woman. They don't understand that a man is supposed to take care of, provide, protect, nurture and respect women, in order to have a woman that treats him with respect and decency. Some men also don't understand that their views towards women are very degrading and surface level, which all assists in women feeling as though submission to men in any capacity is counterproductive. However, if there were both men and women to state and show that men and women are designed to love, respect, cater to, nurture, and work with one another as a team, a lot within our relationships could be resolved and repaired.

See, submission is a collaborative effort by both the man and woman involved in the relationship. Submission is not something that is automatically granted to someone just because of their gender or position in one's life. It has to be earned based upon respect and love. When a man shows that he loves, respects, honors, and takes care of his woman, this will make his woman feel appreciated and valued. In return, that woman would want to be submissive and nurturing towards him. However, when a man is disrespectful, degrading, and/or does not possess leadership type qualities, this makes a woman feel as though he is not someone to submit to.

While submission is often times regarded for women, there are times and places where men are to be more submissive to their women. Many men don't like to acknowledge this aspect of a relationship because it makes him feel inadequate or as though his masculinity is being stripped from him. That sentiment however, couldn't be any further from the truth. The reality is, there will be times in the relationship where a man would need for his woman to take the lead on situations where maybe she is stronger-suited than he, and he will need for her to guide him in the right direction. There will also be times where the man must cater to and be more nurturing to his woman when the time calls for it, and he should not be reluctant to do so.

Just as it should not be regarded as somehow weak, inferior, or degrading for women to be submissive to a good quality man, men should not be considered to be any of those things in regards to good quality women. Relationships are all about balance, and we should not be afraid to balance each other out by taking on certain roles at certain times. Although one may play a role more often than another, this still is apart of duality and a nice healthy balance between men and women.

Its important for me to also point out that there should be no instance where both the man and woman are being submissive or dominant towards one another at the same time, as both of these things would result in non-progressive behaviors and situations. If both the man and woman are being submissive to one another simultaneously, no one would know when to take charge and be proactive, resulting in stagnation and confusion. On the opposite end, if both the man and the woman are being dominant towards one another simultaneously, there would be a battle, which would lead to confrontation and friction, ultimately leading to a break up. This is why it is very important for us to have a

clear and concise understanding as far

as balance in our relationships, to

eliminate as much confusion and

counterproductive behavior as possible.

ESTABLISHING ROLES IN THE

RELATIONSHIP

Now, I do personally feel as

though the man should be in the more

dominant role in the relationship majority

of the time, because by nature, I feel

that is the role that is designated for

him. A man by nature is a leader,

provider, and protector; and by him being in this natural role/element, this will do nothing but bring forth the best attributes of his masculinity. Men being able to fully embrace and tap into their masculinity would result into women being able to fall in line by her tapping into and embracing her femininity which would bring harmony and balance to the male and female interaction and exchange.

A man must embody someone that has control and is able to take care of his household and family, which yet

again will make his female counterpart
fall in line by helping him to maintain the
household and family, and being of
assistance. This dynamic gives a man a
sense of power and purpose, which
gives a need for that man in a woman's
life. Women would then see that the
man is providing her with love, stability,
protection, comfort and other things of
that nature, which would give a woman
a greater incentive to be submissive,
and make sure that she is taking care of
the man that is taking care of *her.*

However, a man cannot abuse his
power and his authority over his woman,

or this will make her want to rebel against him and/or leave. This is why respect and order in the relationship is greatly needed. Neither the man nor the woman, should feel degraded, small, unimportant, and undervalued in the relationship. Both the man and woman should know that both of their positions are important and necessary for the relationship to thrive, grow, and evolve. When roles are established and the understanding and respect of the roles are made clear, this will eliminate any competition, confusion, or power-trips.

I know that there will be many *"independent women that don't need a man"*, and plenty of *"weak-minded 50-50 beta males"* that will have a problem with what I said as far as the structure of how the relationship should be with the man being the provider and the woman being of assistance to him. But those of us that truly want healthy, long-lasting, peaceful, relationships with order to them, know and understand that this is a way to achieve such a dynamic. Men need to be in their natural roles as protectors and providers, so that they can be the best versions of their

masculine selves; and women need to

be in the nurturing, supportive role to

really be more in tune with their feminine

selves.

With this set up, there would be

hardly any friction, confrontation, or

competition between the man and the

woman in the relationship because both

parties would be in alignment with

nature. Confrontation, friction, or

competition, only results when you have

both the man and the woman competing

for the same position within the

relationship, making it much more

complicated to collaborate in a loving,

and effective manner.

Now, there are plenty of couples

out there that feel as though being in a

50/50 relationship as far as the roles,

duties, and responsibilities are

concerned is the better option because

it gives both parties equality in the

relationship. And while I can understand

and respect this attempt at duality, you

must know that this set-up most times

still contributes to the " battle of the

sexes" where no one wants to truly &

fully cater or submit. *How?* Well

because in the 50/50 set-up, everybody feels entitled to get their way due to having equal "skin in the game", thus making them feel like *why should I cater to you when I do the same things that you do?"*

So if you are a "50/50" type of guy that is looking for a woman to submit and cater to you, you must know that it will never happen to the extent that you would like because she will see you as her help-mate and not someone that is carrying the kingdom. On the other hand, if you are a 50/50 type of woman, you will never truly feel your most feminine self, because in this dynamic,

you are playing a masculine role of also

being the provider and protector which

may lead to you feeling as though your

man is really not that much deserving of

you being the submissive more

nurturing type. Your man may also stop

viewing you as a more feminine being

and not treat you with the more tender

love and care that you naturally need

due to him seeing you in that more

masculine position on a subconscious

level.

Again, I do feel as though the male should play the more masculine role of the provider and protector, and the woman should play the more submissive, catering role, in the relationship. Neither party should feel somehow disrespected, overwhelmed, or offended for the positions that they play for majority or some of the time. A woman should have no problem with her man taking on the more dominant role for majority of the time, because she should know and understand that this is the role that is better fit for him naturally, and should never challenge this position. If ever a woman has a problem with her man taking on the more dominant role in the relationship of that of a leader, provider, and protector, this speaks more about her character & judgment than anything else. Why? Because it would showcase that she either does not know how to choose a trustworthy man that has such capabilities to take care of and guide her and her family in the right direction, or that she has a misguided or toxic way of dealing with or viewing the less dominant more submissive role in a relationship.

Many women don't know and understand that it takes a lot of wisdom, love, trust, and strength to be submissive in the first place. It requires one to use their better judgment to be able to differentiate between who is a weak leader, and who is a wise and strong leader to be submissive towards. This is not a job for the faint of heart and unwise. Being faint of heart and unwise will lead to a woman being weak and/or choosing a man that is not fit to take care of her and her family in the healthiest way possible.

Only a true Queen knows how to scope out a King that is worthy and wise enough to take control and build, so that she can fall into her natural role and position of a Queen, and be able to effectively cater to the King of her castle, take care of the castle and the family. While this does not relieve the man of his duties to be there for and take care of his castle and family, it does make it a lot easier for him to do. And while the Man is taking care of the providing and protecting areas of the relationship, it does not relieve the woman of her obligations to contribute as well. It only makes it a lot easier for her to do and manage.

See, I'm not opposed to a woman being able to "add to the pot" that her man already has cooking. I understand that we live in a day and age where both the man and the woman enjoy being able to work and make their own monetary contributions to the relationship. However, the fact remains that this should primarily be the man's territory and focus. Whatever the woman is able to scramble up to bring home, should only be a bonus and go towards savings, investing, or other miscellaneous things that the couple agrees is feasible and reasonable to do. It should never be a woman's job *permanently/primarily* to provide for the household. That is the job of the man/ king of the castle.

On the other hand, the man should not solely leave the raising of the children or the upkeep of the house on the woman. While it is the woman's role primarily, a man should still be involved. The main objective is to lighten each other's loads by playing our own natural positions, and not competing and

stepping on one another's toes.

Men and Women should always

operate from a place of love, balance,

patience, and understanding. Never

should there be an instance where one

feels unneeded, under-valued,

unappreciated, and out of place. A man

should always feel as though his home

is his sanctuary, and his woman is his

peace, just as a woman should always

feel as though her man is her protector,

provider, and her safe-haven. We can

both do this by showing one another

respect and appreciation for our

contributions to the relationship instead of throwing in one's face our importance and their shortcomings.

In a perfect world, men and women would have no issues with showing one another gratitude for one's roles, and not belittling one another in attempts to make ourselves feel important. Unfortunately, we live in a world where that is not the case. I believe it has become the norm for men and women to be at odds with one another, because we have gotten out of alignment with the natural order of things, and live in a world that is more competitive than complimentary. This competitive behavior and energy that we all have in attempts to adapt with the world and society around us, has now trickled over into our relationships, and make us to be combative and demeaning towards the people we are supposed to be loving and building with. In our everyday lives, we are surrounded by a world where we have to be cut-throat and over-powering in order to get ahead, and it bleeds over into our home life and relationships. It has become so embedded into us that we don't know how or when to turn it off.

Your marriage or relationship is never the place to try to destroy, divide, over-power, and conquer. It's a place where you should come together and unite as one unit, and leave that competitive nature for the outside world.

The bottom line is, we lack an understanding of each other as far as men and women, and we need to understand that we are made to compliment each other and build. Not compete with one another and destroy.

MEN'S ISSUES WITH FINDING

SUBMISSIVE WOMEN

So many men come to me

feeling like everything as far as building

with a woman, or finding a feminine

woman to build with, is a lost cause.

They feel as though women that are

feminine, loving, supportive, and

submissive, no longer exist in today's

society. This is due largely in part to

social media, and the social climate in

general, that is teaching women that in

order for her to be a "Boss Chick", she

must adopt the same toxic and destructive qualities of the men that she is trying so desperately to avoid.

These qualities consist of being degrading, placing themselves on pedestals, becoming overly self-centered and selfish, and neglecting everybody else's thoughts, feelings, and emotions that don't feed into their egos. With this type of attitude that is possessed by the majority of women, it makes it extremely difficult for men to become romantically involved, let alone approach a woman.

The reality is, there are a lot of women that don't desire to be in relationships where they are not in the dominant role. They want to be the providers, the bread-winners, and the Kings. Anything other than that, they view as weak or inferior, and that's the last thing a damaged woman wants to feel. Thus, they look for subpar men that they can control so they can feel empowered and needed.

This is a dangerous game to play. Little do many of these women know, is that one day, that *"subpar", "controlled"* man, will begin to feel emasculated and leave her for a woman that holds him in a higher regard. Men need to feel needed, and once he does not feel that, it's only a matter of time before he strays away. Taking care of a man and treating him like your son, goes against the natural laws of nature and eats away at his masculinity. Real men need to be providers and protectors in order to feel like he is fulfilling his purpose in life. Even if at one time he felt as if this set-up of having his woman play the more masculine role was fine, he will

eventually wake up from this slumber

and begin to feel inadequate and either

start to question his importance, cheat,

or leave.

Now, there are many instances

where men are comfortable with their

woman playing the dominant role and

taking care of them. Most of these men

that feel this way, however, have not yet

fully grown into their manliness and

have not witnessed a true masculine,

alpha male in action. They probably

grew up in a single-mother household

where they have grown accustomed to having women take care of and coddle them. But women must understand that these men will never make her feel her true feminine self.

Women subconsciously or even consciously, need to be and feel provided for and protected by their man. When they do not, they will feel this constant void or emptiness within their relationship which may also cause her to seek it outside of the relationship, or belittle the man that she's with because she will view him as less than.

This is why men should never be content with their women taking on the role of provider and protector, because it is unnatural to who and what she is, which will cause her to act other than her true feminine self. Real feminine women, no matter how "strong" or powerful she is, knows that her true strength and power is in her ability to nurture and be of assistance to a strong, dominant, intelligent man. She knows that finding a man that is fit to take care of her and be the one in "control", helps to free up her time to take care of not only herself, but ultimately her household and her man. When both parties are taking care of what they need to take care of, they are both put at ease and much happier within their relationships.

Men need to try their best to stay, and be in a dominant and powerful position. This gives you necessity, purpose, and dignity as a man. Women that are submissive, nurturing, and of great support, will naturally be attracted to you because she will see you as a leader, provider, & protector, which makes you an asset to her. When your woman views you as an asset, she will do whatever is in her power to keep you satisfied; which mostly requires her to be submissive.

As you can see, submission goes back to balance and reciprocation. No one is dictating or ruling over someone else out of force, but rather giving out of love, understanding, and appreciation.

BRIDGING THE GAP OF CONFUSION

There's many men and women that want or require certain things in relationships, but fail to realize this balance and reciprocal element that I have mentioned, which does nothing but make them become even more bitter,

angry, or discouraged when it comes to

building solid relationships. So many

times I hear men say things like "I need

a submissive woman that will listen to

me and cater to me."; all the while he is

not a provider, protector, leader, or

nurturer in any capacity. Then there's

those women that say "I need a man

that can spoil me and take care of me";

all the while she is doing nothing that's

even remotely deserving of such

treatment.

We cannot be out here having

these high expectations and demands

for what we want and need from a significant other, when we ourselves are not ready and willing to step up and do what is required to attract and get that type of individual to build with. If we want something, we must first showcase our significance and worthiness. Otherwise, you will continue to run into situation after situation where you feel like you are not getting the type of man or woman that you need.

The irony of building solid relationships is the fact that it always goes back to self. We must work on who we are as individuals first, so that we know exactly what type of person we are in our rawest form. Once we do this, we will learn our strengths and weaknesses and be able to effectively build on the things that are good quality attributes, and destroy whatever is not conducive to our growth and well-being.

Working on yourself and seeing who you are; even the ugly parts, will help you to be able to be completely honest with yourself so that you can really put in the necessary work to become the best version of yourself that you can possibly be. You will then start to attract the right person to you that you desire. The key though, is not to only work on yourself just to get someone that you are interested in, as this will lead to you not completely and fully dedicating yourself to true self-improvement and elevation. You will instead start to slack off and stop the self-elevation once you feel like you won the "prize".

You must work on yourself for the true purpose of self-elevation and improvement, so that you can attract and accept authentic people into your life that you know are good for you. When you have true self-awareness and enlightenment, it will be hard for

anybody to just come into your life and

knock you off your focus. Why?

Because you know yourself enough to

understand who is a phony, fake, fraud

or user. When you are truly on the

journey to self-improvement everything

and everybody around you will reflect

that, for the most part. In addition to

that, when you are only "faking the funk"

of working on yourself to get someone,

they may very well see through your act

and get turned off and leave you,

anyway.

THE BRUTAL TRUTH

When I tell women things like "*You can very well get a man that loves you, respects you, takes care of you, and caters to you; but you have to be a kind, loving, supportive, submissive woman to obtain that kind of man.*", their mouths automatically scrunch up and their eyes roll into the back of their heads, because they have not been told the truth. They have instead been lied to by other women that have not done their own self-work, and told that they can be the "kingly", "independent", "strong", "dominant", and "aggressive" woman,

---

and get whatever man she so desires. This leads them to think that there is no self-work to be done, and women that think like me are dumb, desperate, and foolish, when in all actuality it's the women like them that are going to be forever searching for a man that does not want her.

A man that is going to be taking care of you, loving you, catering to you, and so forth, is going to expect certain things in return. One of the most common things that kind of man is going to expect is submission from his woman.

That kind of man is not going to tolerate for too long, a woman that is combative, competitive, stubborn, and controlling. He needs a woman that is teachable, understanding, nurturing, and able to take direction. Any woman that feels otherwise must be dealing with weak-minded or weak-spirited type of pushover men, to which she will never feel complete with. Why? Because as I stated before, women subconsciously need strong men that can put her in her place when and if need be. In a loving and healthy way, of course.

I understand that men naturally desire a woman that is submissive and nurturing. They want a woman that they can come home to and she somehow seems to make all of his problems from the outside world melt away. So many men come to me saying that they need to be the leader of their household, but fail to take a look at what they must possess in order to achieve such a role.

Most of the men that are complaining about not having a woman to nurture them or be submissive to them in any way, are not taking care of business as they should. Instead, they are struggling, unsure of who they are, lost, broken, and in many cases looking for a woman to help them with finances and keeping everything afloat. This is a very weak mindset and position to be in, which is why they are more than likely finding themselves feeling unappreciated and passed over by the women that they would like to be with.

The type of women that are going to be patient, loving, kind, submissive, nurturing, supportive, and understanding, are going to need a man that can hold it down on his own. A man's ability to be a provider and protector shows that he is a true leader and stable, which is what is going to attract this kind of woman to you. A man showcasing that he is unstable, broken in all aspects of the word, and struggling horribly, will do nothing but get passed up by the good quality woman that he is seeking, every time. She will instead go after the man that may not be the richest, cutest, or even the most intelligent, but he does embody the leader, provider, and protector qualities that most women are needing from a man.

Many men that I tell this to start to say things like *"all women are gold-diggers"*, but this is not true. The truth of the matter is that women naturally look for men that are stable and that can provide for them. When a man does not understand this, most times he is the type of man that does not have his life together and does not want to put in the necessary work to take care of his household. He is instead looking for a woman to live off of, or just wants to do enough to get by. This in and of itself is 9/10 why he is having difficulty finding a good mate that would indeed have no problem submitting to him, and catering to him. The reality of the situation is, he is not worth it.

Many men need to get on their grind and stop whining about having to be a man. A major part of being a man is being able to hold down your castle and keep everything in order and smooth sailing. Life is difficult for everyone, I know; but that should never be an excuse to slack off and complain about doing whatever is in your power to take care of your duties and obligations as a man. As long as it is done in a

righteous way, of course.

What men fail to realize is, it

makes him stick out among the rest

when women see him working hard and

making things happen regardless of the

obstacles, & is very much so attractive.

Women love to see a man that is

resilient and reliable. Showcasing the

fact that you don't mind working hard to

make sure everything is going well for

yourself and your family, is a quality and

a trait that majority of all women will

respect and appreciate, making her not

mind being nurturing and submissive to you.

Ladies and gentlemen, to sum everything up, submission is not the enemy, and is also not something that is freely given. It is a key ingredient to a healthy relationship between two people that truly love and respect one another. Submission is a key component in a dynamic where both parties understand how it is supposed to be used, and should never be abused in any way. A woman should never use submission as something to hold over her man's head in order to get her way, and it should never be used by a man as a way to control and be abusive to his woman. Both parties must use submission in a healthy and caring way.

When it comes to healthy relationships and marriages, both the man and woman must view each other as "the prize". Nobody is above or beneath the other. No one is more valuable or more deserving than the other. Both are uniquely beneficial and important. As long as everybody understands this, there should be no problems with being in harmony and balance within our relationships.

Remember, submission is a great thing.

It just has to be given in a relationship

where the person is deserving. So, if

you are in a healthy and loving

relationship, give submission a try and

watch magic happen.

CLOSING:

Women and Men should both be

bringing things of substance and value

to the relationship. Having someone

with morals, goals, values, and interests

that coincide with you and what you

stand for, are a must. No woman should

be getting into a relationship just

because a man has money and power

and no man should get into a

relationship with a woman just because

she is submissive and attractive. It must

go deeper than that. A person's

character, what they are about, what

they stand for, how they treat you, and

what they engage in, should always

reign supreme, although those other

things are important. Too many times I

see men and women get involved into

relationships for surface level reasons,

or out of necessity, and it always ends in

disaster. So always look beyond just the

surface when it comes to finding a

person to build a healthy foundation and

relationship with. I hope this book was

able to give you much more clarity on

balance within relationships, especially

in regards to submission and how if

used correctly, can be a beautiful thing.

Peace and much love.

Made in the USA
Columbia, SC
28 September 2023

23550223R00048